## The Duke of Northumberland

*I have real pleasure in welcoming you to Alnwick Castle, and I hope you enjoy your visit. It is a very special place, and your money is helping to maintain it in good condition for future generations to enjoy.*

*My family have lived at Alnwick for nearly 700 years, and the castle reflects a history of war and peace, cruelty and benevolence, of artistic patronage, building and innovation on a scale to rival any house in Britain. Thankfully it is also a wonderful family home and I have always loved it, probably because I was born here, in one of the bedrooms. As children, my brothers, sisters and I treated it as a huge playroom, not appreciating the priceless paintings and furniture that were often targets for water pistols and arrows! Thank goodness it is still a home, where children can play (albeit with anxious parents fearful of costly damage).*

*Over the years my wife and I hope to extend the range of your tour of Alnwick, so please come back and see how we are getting on.*

*Northumberland*

# ALNWICK CASTLE

## Home of the Duke of Northumberland

# CONTENTS

*Changes may be made within the rooms and to items on display.*
*Restricted opening times may apply to particularly light-sensitive rooms, such as the Chapel.*

# The
# CASTLE SITE

*The story of Alnwick Castle* emerges in the Norman age. *At that time many motte and bailey castles appeared in the old Saxon earldom of Northumbria. Layout of the site still carries characteristic features: defensive development on a natural bluff above a river, a defensive bailey within the line of an outer ditch and the creation of an impregnable motte within the line of an inner ditch. Today, these form the outer bailey, inner bailey and keep of the castle.*

Next was the building of a 'shell-keep' in stone which developed as a series of semi-circular towers linked by curtain walls around an inner courtyard. The Norman chevron design decorating the archway of the keep's gatehouse (pictured right) is of the first part of the 12th century; so too are the small regularly shaped square stones to be found in stretches of the curtain walls (north side outer bailey; east side inner bailey).

NORMAN CHEVRON DECORATION
OF THE GATEWAY TO THE KEEP

LOOKING WEST ACROSS THE INNER BAILEY TOWARDS THE KEEP; TO THE RIGHT, THE POSTERN TOWER, CONSTABLE'S TOWER AND HOTSPUR'S SEAT

A chronicler described the castle as being 'most heavily fortified' in 1138. The builder of this fortress was the Norman magnate Eustace who had grown powerful in the service of King Henry I and through marriage to the heiress of Yves de Vescy. Eustace's descendants adopted the Vescy surname. The great Alnwick barony, of which the castle was head, provided the crown with a dozen knights.

GATEWAY TO THE
ALNWICK GARDEN

At this time Alnwick lay within the overlap of the feudal powers of the English and Scottish kings. In the 12th century it came into the English orbit and this threatened the political independence of the Vescys. Hostility between the magnate Eustace de Vescy and King John, who visited Alnwick on his tour of his northern borders, stemmed from royal encroachment of power.

POSTERN TOWER,
WATERCOLOUR BY
D. MOSSMAN, c. 1860

Details of the castle site as seen today emerged in the first half of the 14th century, shortly after the castle's acquisition by the first Percy lord of Alnwick in 1309. The barbican, Alnwick's most distinctive military feature, was added to the castle's entrance to provide an outer defence and to protect the gatehouse, another 14th century feature. The outer bailey was equipped with a series of strong towers, the largest being the Abbot's Tower at the exposed north-western angle. These towers were interspersed at intervals by the smaller *guerites* or watch-towers built on the heads of curtain walls.

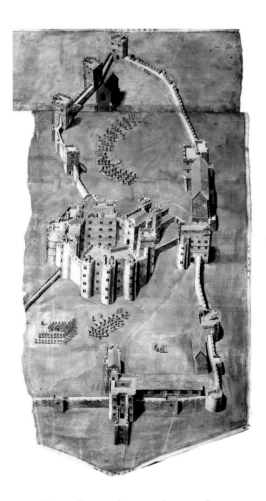

THOMAS TRESWELL'S PLAN OF ALNWICK CASTLE
IN THE EARLY 17TH CENTURY

The middle gateway was also built then. The 14th century pattern of defences in the inner bailey was similar to those of the outer bailey: the curtain wall is punctuated with towers and *guerites*. The Postern Tower provided another exit from the castle. Sorties could be made through the Postern gate to prevent attempts by besiegers to mine under the wall of the keep on its exposed north flank.

The final Percy embellishment of this recently acquired fortress was the addition of semi-circular towers to the shell-keep and the building of the pair of octagonal towers onto the keep's gatehouse. The heraldic shields of arms decorating the tops of the gatehouse towers link their building to the second Percy lord.

Additional buildings and structures, since gone, are described in written and pictorial sources. Thomas Treswell's plan of the early 17th century shows ranges of stable buildings and an exchequer house next to the gatehouse in the outer bailey as well as a chapel, pant and additional tower standing in the inner bailey. Peter Hartover's painting (late 17th century) shows the chapel in ruins and provides a good elevation of the exchequer house. Written evidence as early as 1314 lists the strength of the garrison: 3 knights, 38 fully armed soldiers and no less than 40 'hoblars', mounted troopers, who formed the backbone of the military force on the borders with Scotland.

THE OCTAGONAL TOWERS AT THE
ENTRANCE TO THE KEEP

A survey of 1538 reveals the daily routine of the castle's garrison who had within the castle walls a bakehouse, brewhouse, military storehouse, cart sheds and stabling for 160 horses. A blacksmith's shop was conveniently situated immediately outside the barbican. The straight stretch of highway from the barbican through Bailiffgate and Ratten Row provided the garrison horses with an exercise ground. In 1538 the castle needed a new drawbridge, 'an iron yett' or gate for the gatehouse, the replacement of roofing leads and gutters and repairs to the curtain walls and one of the towers.

HERALDIC SHIELDS
AND MEDIEVAL STONE
FIGURES STILL STAND
GUARD ON THE
OCTAGONAL TOWERS

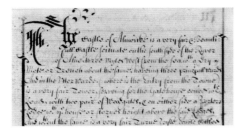

DESCRIPTION OF
ALNWICK CASTLE
1586

A later survey provides additional domestic details. The inner bailey contained a small garden, a horse mill (necessary in times of siege), a chantry and school served by a friar and, on the south wall, a set of garderobes, or lavatories, which emptied into the Bowburn stream.

The castle then had two prisons: one at the gatehouse, the other at the base of the northern octagonal tower where there still survives a dungeon or *oubliette*, into which prisoners could be lowered and kept in confinement.

Subsequently, when the castle was for a time in royal hands, it was written off in defensive terms: it was 'not liable to abide the force of any shot or to hold out any time if it should be assaulted'. Thereafter it developed its importance as the administrative centre of a great barony and the extensive Percy estates. Control of the castle lay in the hands of its constable. The earl's chief officers, his receivers and auditors, came twice a year to collect rents and fines using the Auditor's Tower and the exchequer house at Alnwick Castle. The rent days' takings filled saddlebags which were carried on packhorses, under armed escort, to the earl's counting house in London.

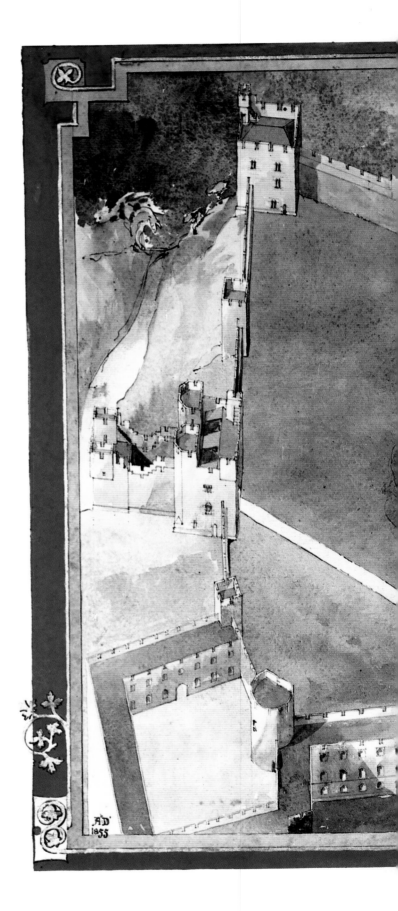

AN ARTIST'S IMPRESSION OF
HOTSPUR FOR THE ROYAL
SHAKESPEARE COMPANY, 1946

ISOMETRIC PLAN OF ALNWICK CASTLE, WATERCOLOUR BY F.R.WILSON, 1855

ESPERANCE EN DIEV

WILLIAM THE
LION MONUMENT

RIGHT: MILITARY ARTIFACTS
ARE ON DISPLAY IN THE
PERCY TENANTRY
VOLUNTEERS EXHIBITION IN
THE CONSTABLE'S TOWER

# ALNWICK CASTLE
## *in* HISTORY

*In 1093 Malcolm Canmore, King of the Scots, son of Duncan and defeater of Macbeth, was killed just north of the castle across the River Aln. In 1140 another Scottish king, William the Lion, was captured just off the west of the castle. These events of the early Norman period are connected with the claims of the Scottish kings to territories of the pre-Conquest earldom of Northumbria. Both kings were making sorties to test the feudal opposition. In 1773 the First Duchess set up a monument to Malcolm from whom she claimed descent. A memorial at the gatehouse to Hulne Park records William's capture.*

LADY ELIZABETH SEYMOUR WHO BECAME FIRST DUCHESS
PAINTED BY ALLAN RAMSAY C.1740

During the Wars of the Roses Alnwick kept changing hands and, by the end of 1462, had come under siege by Yorkist forces. The castle was manned mainly by a contingent of French gunners who made their escape through the Postern Tower to join a relieving Lancastrian force. Before they fled they poured their cannonballs down the castle well. Some of these, recovered in the course of the 18th century castle restoration, are now on display in the dungeon.

The Civil War (1642–1650) brought problems to Alnwick. The Cromwellian soldiers burned down the township of Walkergate just outside the castle walls. Troopers were billeted in the castle and the surrounding districts. Complaints were made about the commandeering of horses, fodder and food supplies. Rents were difficult to gather and transport to London which meant a period of uncertain income for the earl.

In September 1650, after the Battle of Dunbar, 6000 Scottish prisoners were lodged for one night 'betwixt the middle and upper gate' of Alnwick castle on their way south to Durham.

Lodging at the castle of a totally different kind took place in the Second World War. Girls from Newcastle Church High School were evacuated to the castle and shared the facilities of the local Duchess's High School for Girls. From 1945, former servants' quarters provided accommodation, first for an emergency teachers training college, then, from 1949–1977, Alnwick College of Education. From 1981 to the present day this part of the castle has been used by American students of St. Cloud State University, Minnesota.

MALCOLM'S CROSS

# *Castle*
# RESTORATIONS

*During the 17th century and the first half of the 18th century the castle was in decay and the landed estate provided income but no amenity. Parts of the castle were even being leased to local town craftsmen. Canaletto's romantic view of the castle, 1752, barely masks the forlorn state of the fabric.*

Division of Percy lands in 1750 meant that the estates in Yorkshire, Cumberland and Sussex were separated from those in Northumberland. The inheritors of these northern lands concentrated their attention on Alnwick. This castle became the absorbing passion of the heiress Elizabeth Seymour, descendant of the Percys, who together with her husband Hugh, first Earl (1750) then Duke of Northumberland (1766), set about turning a derelict castle into their principal country seat. The castle could offer so little in the way of comfort on their first visit in 1751 that the couple had to stay in the old exchequer house!

CANALETTO WAS ALSO COMMISSIONED TO PAINT SYON HOUSE (BELOW) IN 1749 AND NORTHUMBERLAND HOUSE, LONDON (ABOVE LEFT) IN 1752

HUGH SMITHSON AND ELIZABETH SEYMOUR
THE FIRST DUKE AND DUCHESS OF NORTHUMBERLAND

# The PERCYS & ALNWICK

## From the Norman Conquest to the Battle of Shrewsbury 1066–1403

*William de Percy (d.1096), founder of this family, came to England with William the Conqueror. He came from the Caen region of the Norman duchy where villages still bear the name 'Perci'. He was in the war band of Hugh of Avranches who became Earl of Chester. William took his share of the Norman division of lands and became settled as a magnate in Yorkshire where he held lands of the king, the Earl of Chester and the Bishop of Durham. William reformed the old Saxon abbey of Whitby, Yorkshire, and joined the Crusade, on which venture he died.*

In the mid-12th century the heiress **Agnes Percy (d.1204)** married Jocelin of Louvain, brother of the wife of the Norman king Henry I . Their figures decorated every Percy pedigree reminding the family of the importance of this marriage alliance.

In the political turmoil of the 13th century the Percys found themselves, like so many other barons, opposed to King John: **Richard Percy (d.1244)** was one of the twenty five magnates appointed to oversee the provisions of Magna Charta. But in the middle of the 13th century the Percy lord was not persuaded by the baronial party of Simon de Montfort and remained royalist. Loyalty and continued service both in council and under arms later recommended Percy when King Edward I pursued his cause in Scotland.

**Henry Percy (1273–1314)**, the first lord of Alnwick, appeared the ideal servant of Plantagenet kingship: warrior against the Scots, Keeper of the Marches, he was also a member of the King's Council and acted as regent in the king's absence. He was summoned to the king's parliament as baron by writ. Who better then to control the great and strategically important northern barony of Alnwick than this loyal Percy? This old Vescy barony had come under the control of Antony Bec, the powerful Bishop of Durham, who threatened to absorb it into the palatinate lands which would mean its loss to royal control. However, Bec was

persuaded to sell the barony to Henry Percy and the deal was sealed with royal approval in 1309.

In the 14th century the Percys could do no wrong. **Henry, second lord of Alnwick (1314–1352)**, like his father, spent a lifetime consumed in negotiating with the Scots and guarding the Border. His reward was the consolidation of his Northumberland lands: the barony of Warkworth and the lordships of Rothbury and Newburn were granted to him. He helped defeat the Scots at Neville's Cross (1346). The Percy power base came to shift northwards from Yorkshire to Northumberland. Both Henry and his son and successor were buried at the abbey of Alnwick rather than at one of their endowed Yorkshire abbeys.

Political power continued to increase. **Henry Percy (1368–1408)**, whose father had fought at Crécy, warred in France but became increasingly caught up in politics at home. He became Marshal of England (1376) and was created Earl of Northumberland at the coronation of Richard II (1377).

An image of Henry, the First Earl, from a manuscript in the British Museum

It is believed that the use of the crescent in the Percy badge dates from this time: it had once been the badge of the old Saxon earldom of Northumbria. This advancement came not long after a marriage to a widow and heiress who brought two more great northern baronies, those of Prudhoe and Cockermouth, to the family. This consolidated the primacy of the Percys in the Borders.

Increased power was soon used to try to broker kingship: Richard II was forced to stand down and Henry IV set up in his place. When this king no longer suited, then rebellion was resorted to in an attempt to overthrow him. But defeats at Shrewsbury (1403) and Bramham Moor (1406) brought an end to the Percys' grip on political power.

Most famous of all Percys, **Harry 'Hotspur' (b.1364 d.1403)** emerged during this period. He is Alnwick's own hero for he was born here at the castle, in the quarters above the gatehouse of the keep. His nickname, 'Hotspur', sums up his quicksilver temperament, courage and impetuousness. He was raised in the tradition of his ancestors. He battled in the Borders; undertook crusade in the marches of eastern Europe; fought on land and sea against France. He was the hero of the chronicler Froissart who relates the quarrel between Douglas the Scot and Hotspur which led to the midnight battle of Otterburn (1388), an event which showed the deep rooted dynastic rivalries of late medieval society. Hotspur was taken prisoner yet his courage was the stuff of heroes.

FIGURE WITH PERCY HERALDIC EMBLEMS FROM MEDIEVAL WOOD CARVING WRESSEL CASTLE, YORKSHIRE

Hotspur's own squire John Harding was his greatest admirer. Harding wrote a history of England which in its account of the 14th and 15th centuries was a story of the greatness, bravery and service to the crown of the Percys. Harding, writing in the mid-15th century, beseeched the king to take note that the Percys held 'the hearts of the people by North and ever had'. Harding had his old master Hotspur in mind. No wonder Shakespeare was so fascinated by Hotspur! The sub-title of his play *'Henry IV Part I '* was after all the *'Life and Death of Henry surnamed Hotspur'*.

# The Percys and Alnwick 1403-1750

In two hundred years following Hotspur's death at the Battle of Shrewsbury (1403) only two Percy earls died in their beds. Of the others, three were killed in battle, two executed and two murdered.

Hotspur's son, **Henry the Second Earl (1403–1455),** loyal to Henry V who restored him, was a patron of learning, endowing fellowships at Oxford and establishing a chantry and school at the castle. He also built Bondgate Tower at the southern entrance to the town. He died in battle fighting for the Lancastrian cause as did his son, the **Third Earl (1455–1461). The Fourth Earl (1461–1489)** gained notoriety for his allegiance to the cause of Richard III, his failure to intervene in the Yorkist cause at Bosworth Field and his murder by peasantry for his zealousness in collecting taxes for the first Tudor monarch.

**The Fifth Earl (1489–1527)** was a great courtier at a time when the Tudor court was absorbed in Renaissance magnificence. He escorted the Princess Margaret, daughter of Henry VII, in great pomp and splendour northwards to her marriage with the Scottish king James IV: in the parks at Alnwick the princess shot a deer. No more detailed account survives of the daily life of a great Tudor lord than is provided by this earl's Household Book. The splendour of his own household came close to that of the king; its expense crippled his estates.

The character of his son **Henry the Sixth Earl (1527-1537),** is intriguing. This Henry was the victim of the powerful central government of Henry VIII. Against the new men who served the king, the old nobility with their old religious faith stood no chance. Henry's fate is made all the more poignant because of his personal circumstances. He was brought up as a page in the household of Cardinal Wolsey yet it fell his lot to arrest Wolsey for the king; he fell in love with Anne Boleyn and wanted to wed her yet he had to stand aside for the sake of the king. In the end, childless, unhappy and dismayed with his brothers' political entanglements, he put his lands into the hands of a king who had caused him and his family so much grief..

ILLUMINATED INITIAL FROM ANNE BOLEYN'S PERSONAL PRAYER BOOK IN ALNWICK CASTLE LIBRARY

Just when the fortunes of the Percys seemed well and truly sunk, a change of monarch brought about their restoration. The accession of Mary brought the restoration of **Thomas Percy Seventh Earl (1557–1572)** to his earldom and his ancestral lands in 1557. There was optimism that he could weld together all those parts of the old local community in his northern barony which had been destroyed or broken down in the turbulence of the times. The earl was urged to take up residence at Alnwick.

Instead, in Queen Elizabeth's reign, he chose the desperate course of rebellion for the old faith and for Mary Queen of Scots and lost all in the chaotic 'Rebellion of the Northern Earls', as his escapade with the Earl of Westmorland was called. Alnwick witnessed the sad spectacle of the Seventh Earl being brought back a prisoner from Scotland on his journey to trial and execution in York.

Thomas's folly sank the family under a cloud of suspicion for the next half century. Thomas and his brother **Henry**, who in turn became **Eighth Earl (1572–1585)**, were sons of Thomas Percy, a leader in the popular uprising, the Pilgrimage of Grace (1536–1537). Authority was suspicious that Henry espoused the old faith and the cause of the Scottish queen and so he was imprisoned in the Tower of London where he was found dead, most probably murdered.

Little did **Henry the Ninth Earl (1585–1632)** imagine on his succession to his father that imprisonment in the Tower would be his fate too. Henry followed the course of a true Renaissance nobleman. To whatever interest he turned, he gave his full intellectual attention: military tactics; astronomy and navigation; science, particularly alchemy; surveying and cartography. There is little wonder that this nobleman accumulated one of the greatest libraries of his day; was known as the 'Wizard Earl'; patronised scholars and was a friend of Sir Walter Raleigh,

through whom he was able to savour the products of the New World.

SIR WALTER RALEIGH'S NAME ON A LIST OF GUESTS OF THE NINTH EARL, WITH POTATOES ON THE MENU, 1591

But, at the height of his success when his support for James of Scotland as monarch to follow Elizabeth brought him even greater influence and wealth, misfortune struck. Important among the Earl's servants was the constable of Alnwick Castle who had local responsibility for administering the castle and barony, controlling bailiffs and collecting rents. The castle constable was the Ninth Earl's distant cousin, Thomas. Thomas was a useful tool in the earl's affairs, particularly well placed to be his messenger to the Scottish court. But he also abused his office, exploited tenants and pocketed moneys. At Syon, the Earl's Middlesex house, Thomas Percy dined with his master on the evening of the 4th November 1605. The next day the plot to blow up the Houses of Parliament was discovered: Thomas Percy was one of the principal gunpowder plotters and was shot dead making his escape in the Midlands.

THOMAS PERCY SEVENTH EARL (1557–1572)

Though pleading his innocence, the Earl was arrested and confined to the Tower of London where he spent the next 17 years. He was fined a massive sum of £30,000 which indeed forced the Earl to increase the efficiency of his estates so as to raise money to pay it off. In the Tower he suffered no physical hardship: he chose his diet, modified his apartments to his needs, improved the walks, had his gardening done by his Syon gardener, administered his lands, educated his children and met up again with his great friend Raleigh! The Ninth Earl was the last Percy for four centuries to be born in Northumberland. On his release from the Tower he was confined to his Sussex estate.

THE SIGNATURE OF THOMAS PERCY – ONE OF THE MAIN COLLABORATORS IN THE GUNPOWDER PLOT, 1605

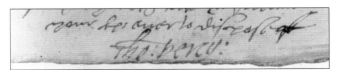

His son **Algernon Tenth Earl (1632-1668)** only visited Alnwick, as he did in 1640, when matters of state brought him to the North. This Earl learned the lesson of his father's predicament and in the turbulent times of the Civil War steered a very judicious course. He held high office under Charles I being Lord High Admiral and President of the Council of War but held back from full commitment to the royalist cause and so lost his commands. He supported a compromise between king and people which established his reputation for impartiality. After the king was arrested and imprisoned he was made Governor of the Royal Children, who lived at the Earl's house at Syon.

Remarkably the Earl brought his vast lands, including Alnwick, through the Civil War still intact. Algernon was a great patron of artists but his collection of silver and many of his fine old master paintings had to be sold to bear the costs of the times. After this, family involvement with Alnwick declined.

**The Eleventh Earl (1668-1670)** died young while on Grand Tour and his only child, the heiress Elizabeth, had to fight off the claims of others to her lands and titles. Her marriage to Charles Seymour, Sixth Duke of Somerset, in 1682 brought control of the estates to a man whose interest lay in

court, collecting and horse racing. So long as his estates provided for his interests he was not much troubled. It was only when his son Algernon Seymour reigned briefly as the **Seventh Duke of Somerset (1748-1750)**, that interest in Percy ancestry was once more rekindled.

ELIZABETH PERCY, SIXTH
DUCHESS OF SOMERSET,
(b.1667 d.1722)
BY HENRI GASCARS

## The Percys and Alnwick 1750-Present

Enthusiasm for Percy ancestry very quickly and readily rubbed off onto Algernon Seymour's daughter, the heiress **Elizabeth Seymour**. It was she who brought her family back to Alnwick when this portion of the Percy inheritance came to her.

Fascinated by her Northern origins and her 'braw rough ancestors' as she called them, she was overwhelmed by the *gothick* atmosphere of the north. For her, Alnwick was a place to enjoy. She breathed new life into its ancient customs, admired its scenery, entertained its worthies and

ALGERNON TENTH EARL
BY SIR ANTHONY VAN DYCK

attended its theatre. Her husband, the Yorkshire man **Hugh Smithson, Earl and First Duke of Northumberland (1750-1786)**, boosted the local economy and secured influence and patronage by restoring the castle and parkland.

He modernised the local agriculture and industries, including coalmining and glass-making on the Tyne. Elizabeth Seymour and her Duke were encouraged by their chaplain Thomas Percy who provided the Duchess with the details of her pedigree and the history of her ancestors. Such was the impact that Elizabeth Seymour had on Alnwick and its environs that, after her death in 1776, her Duke erected monuments to her memory on the estate, including a tower at Brizlee, an observatory at Ratcheugh and a garden house at Hulne Priory.

Elizabeth's son, **Hugh Second Duke (1786-1817)** inherited her enthusiasm for the north. He was the first Percy in centuries to overwinter at Alnwick and set a pattern of management on his estates the influence of which can still be felt. As a lad of 16 he raised a company of recruits from Alnwick to serve in the army with him in the Seven Years War (1756-1763). He became a general in the War of American Independence (1775-1783) and there learned lessons of tactics which he put to good use when he raised his own local volunteers in the Napoleonic conflict. The Fifth Regiment of Foot took the title 'Northumberland Fusiliers' in recognition of his compassion for his men when he was its colonel in Ireland and America. His farming tenants, too, recognised his help and concern when they erected the Tenantry Column at Alnwick in 1816 to celebrate his reign.

**Hugh Third Duke (1817–1847)** consolidated his father's work and expanded the estates. With his Duchess, Charlotte Florentia, he served both country and local community. He was royal representative in both France and Ireland and his Duchess was Governess to Princess Victoria.

No Percy has benefited the castle, estate and local community more than **Algernon Fourth Duke (1847–1865)** who restored the castle. He was already a man of mature judgement and independent outlook when he succeeded his brother the Third Duke. He had served as midshipman and naval officer in the Napoleonic Wars, after which he became immersed in travel and archaeological exploration. He was one of the first Englishmen to journey to Upper Egypt to record Pharoanic remains there. He was a particularly enlightened landowner who provided well for his dependants in the countryside while also making his possessions an amenity for the wider community to enjoy. In 1851 he sent his own estate workmen to see the Great Exhibition and opened Northumberland House and Syon House to the public. He enjoyed the company of enlightened, open-minded men who shared his enthusiasm for art, architecture and archaeology. His reign was a celebration of independent thought and taste mixed with great compassion: no wonder he was known as Algernon 'the Good'!

**George Fifth Duke (1865–1867),** Algernon's cousin and grandson of the First Duke's younger son, succeeded in 1865 at the great age of 87. His son **Algernon Sixth Duke (1867–1899)**, who married Louisa, heiress of

Henry Drummond, banker, political philosopher and religious reformer, was a prominent member of the Catholic Apostolic movement which flourished in the high church atmosphere of Victorian England. Both he and

**Henry Seventh Duke (1899–1918)** were active politicians and courtiers who benefited the local community of Alnwick through their establishment of a workingmen's club and bath houses. The Seventh Duke was a keen local historian who undertook excavation of the castle's barbican ditch.

**Alan Ian Eighth Duke (1918–1930)** was a career soldier

who served in South Africa, the Sudan and throughout the First World War. His Duchess, Helen, who served Queen Elizabeth for many years as her Mistress of the Robes, guided the family through the 1930s and the Second World War in which **George Ninth Duke (1930–1940)** was killed.

The long reign of **Hugh Tenth Duke (1940–1988)** provided the Percy family and estates with

great stability in a period of post-war uncertainty and latterly modern-day prosperity. He transformed his estates to meet changing requirements of the second half of the 20th century. It was Duke Hugh and his Duchess Elizabeth, who decided to make Alnwick Castle their permanent home and the estates their main interest. The Duke was recognised as a foremost agriculturist of his day. His deep interest in science led him to chair the government investigation into bovine foot and mouth disease (1968) and also the Medical Research Council. In 1950 he opened Alnwick Castle to the general public.

**Henry Eleventh Duke (1988–1995)** had a passion for film-making and for the history of his ancestor Hotspur. His brother **Ralph Twelfth Duke (1995)**, who has succeeded him, has concentrated his interests on Alnwick and his northern estates. He is married to Jane Richard and they have four children.

# The HOUSEHOLD

*Some glimpse of the Percy household* is possible from as early as the time young John Harding entered Hotspur's service as a page in 1390. The Household Book of the Fifth Earl in the early 16th century reveals the way a great nobleman and his household lived: food supplies, diet, transport, daily prayers and the hierarchy of servants are all listed.

The household was then continually on the move. Later the earls employed a staff of officers responsible for different aspects of their living: steward of the household, purse bearer, foreign paymaster, clerk of the kitchen, cofferer, gentleman of horse, gentleman usher, disburser for apparel. When the Ninth Earl visited Flanders in 1588, he was accompanied by no fewer than 13 liveried servants.

Lavishness of style persisted into the 18th century. When the First Duchess made her summer stay at Alnwick in 1768 she had a staff of 52 including 11 liveried footmen and 3 liveried stablemen. When the family was absent, the castle household was in the charge of a female housekeeper who was allowed to keep gratuities left by castle visitors. Even when permanent castle staff were on board wages the laundry maids still got their pitcher of ale on washdays!

HOUSEHOLD STAFF IN ATTENDANCE AT ALNWICK CASTLE IN 1908, AT THE TIME OF THE ROYAL VISIT

MRS RENWICK, HOUSEKEEPER, BY OSWALD BIRLEY, 1948

Servants moved around with their masters and came with the dukes to reside at Alnwick in summer. Their mode of travel depended on their station. Some came in advance by coach to prepare, some came with the family by coach and others by the accompanying wagon. A usual way was by ship from London to Alnmouth. The Third Duke sometimes sailed north in his yacht.

HUGH THIRD DUKE OF NORTHUMBERLAND AS PORTRAYED BY RICHARD DIGHTON IN 1832

When resident at the castle, servants abided by house rules which regulated their tasks, their times of work, what and where they ate, when they went to bed. The gate porter kept an eye on male servants who were lodged together in the gatehouse. There was a distinct divide between the upper servants, who included the steward, the clerk of the kitchen, the groom of the chambers, the valet de chambre and the butler, and the rest of the household. But the duke regarded all servants as belonging to his 'family', for each of whom he held himself responsible.

The mid-19th century restoration of the castle had a deep impact on the household. Quarters for stable staff were built at first floor level in the coach yard. House staff were quartered to the south side of the middle gateway where Salvin built a spectacular kitchen with a hydraulic lift capable of raising a ton of coal to fire the roasting spit and ovens. To speed up delivery of food from the kitchen to the State Dining Room, an underground passage was constructed to connect the two. The passage lights at ground level are still visible leading from the area of the middle gateway to the base of the wall of the keep where a pulley wheel indicates the location of the dumb-waiter hoist. The kitchen even employed an engine man!

SERVANTS IN SALVIN'S GREAT KITCHEN, c. 1865

LIVERIED SERVANTS
AT THE CASTLE
A CENTURY AGO

INSTRUCTIONS GIVING AMOUNTS TO BE SPENT ON CHRISTMAS
PRESENTS BY HOUSEHOLD SERVANTS, 1913

Social stability and growing affluence of later Victorian England caused servant numbers to grow. At the end of the 19th century household staff numbered 86. There were 39 women, with 6 laundry-maids, 6 housemaids, 6 kitchen maids as well as personal and travelling maids. Of the 47 men, 4 were footmen and 16 were coachmen and stablemen. Today, under the Household Controller, there are 4 full-time and 9 part-time members of staff.

STAFF AWAITING GUESTS AT A BANQUET IN THE
GUEST HALL TO CELEBRATE THE COMING OF
AGE OF LORD WARKWORTH, 1892

# The INTERIORS

*The style of decoration of Alnwick Castle interiors was the brainchild of the Fourth Duke
and the invention of the Roman architect and archaeologist Luigi Canina (b. 1795 d. 1856).
Canina's professional life had been devoted to restoration work. He met the Duke in Rome in 1853
and discussed the scheme for Alnwick's interior restoration. Prior to this Canina had restored the Villa
Borghese, one of the great 16th century Roman palaces,
after the ravages of the 1848 revolution in Rome.*

Alnwick followed the style of 16th century Roman palaces in its interior decoration. Rome had craftsmen and workshops to provide all decorative skills necessary. Communications by sea and by land were so well developed by mid-19th century that these artefacts in finished form could safely be conveyed all the way from Rome to Alnwick. Distinguished Italian artists and craftsmen were persuaded to participate in the Duke's scheme.

In the end, the Duke decided to create a school of wood carving at Alnwick. Anton Leon Bulletti, a brilliant young Florentine carver, was engaged to come to Alnwick to teach the school. This breathed a new purpose into the restoration work since the object of the school was to provide English carvers with the skills and accomplishments of their continental counterparts.

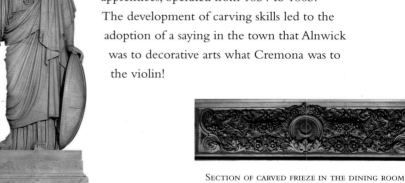

*BRITANNIA* BY GIUSEPPE NUCCI

The carvers' workshops, provided with skylights, were situated in the coach yard. The carving school which was composed of 21 carvers (drawn principally from Glasgow and Newcastle) and 6 apprentices, operated from 1854 to 1863. The development of carving skills led to the adoption of a saying in the town that Alnwick was to decorative arts what Cremona was to the violin!

SECTION OF CARVED FRIEZE IN THE DINING ROOM

Luigi Canina came to Alnwick in 1856 to survey and discuss progress of work with the Duke and British architects who approved the scheme. He was accompanied by his right-hand man Giovanni Montiroli (b. 1817 d. 1888) who was an accomplished draftsman. After Canina's death Montiroli supervised the work both in Rome and at Alnwick. In Rome craftsmen produced the marble fireplaces and balustrades in best Carrara marble. In the workshop of Giovanni Taccalozzi models of the fireplaces made in gesso were first sent to England for the Duke's approval. Italian sculptors of repute carved the statuary figures.

DRAWING ROOM DETAILS

ABOVE LEFT: CARVED WOOD WINDOW SHUTTER
LEFT: MONTIROLI'S CEILING DESIGN, 1856
RIGHT: CARVED MASK OF THE MEDUSA ON DOOR BOSS

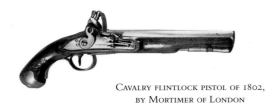

# The
# GUARD CHAMBERS

*Equipment of the Percy Tenantry Volunteers* (1798-1814) - *pistols, powder flasks
and horns, swords and sergeants' pikes - masks the sombreness of this entrance. An exhibition about
these volunteers is displayed in the Constable's Tower.*

## LOWER GUARD CHAMBER

17TH CENTURY BRONZE VENETIAN
DOOR KNOCKER DEPICTING
NEPTUNE STANDING BETWEEN A
SEA-HORSE AND A SEA-UNICORN

AN ARRANGEMENT OF CAVALRY
SWORDS AND POWDER HORNS OF
THE PERCY TENANTRY
VOLUNTEERS

VIEW OF THE GRAND STAIRCASE

SCULPTURE OF LOUISA, SIXTH DUCHESS, BY PIERS CONNOLLY

The statue of the seated figure of Louisa, Sixth Duchess was
sculpted by the North American Piers Connolly,
1869–1871. The figure of *Action* is by John Gott, a British
sculptor who worked in Rome and was patronised by the
Third Duke.

VIEW FROM THE TOP OF THE GRAND STAIRCASE

SUNSET BY CLAUDE LORRAIN
HANGS ABOVE A MID–18TH CENTURY
CARVED GILTWOOD PIER TABLE

The four canvas frieze panels high on the Guard Chamber walls represent scenes from the old border ballad 'Chevy Chase' which tells of a legendary skirmish between Percy and Douglas in the Borders in which both chiefs die. The ballad was edited and published by the First Duke's chaplain Thomas Percy in his *Ancient Reliques of English Poetry* (1765).

'Chevy Chase' is also a Northumbrian pipe-tune. It became the signature tune of the Percy dukes and was played by an ensemble of pipes in the Guard Chamber when welcoming guests to social functions. Paintings in the Guard Chamber include the full length portrait of the Tenth Earl as Lord High Admiral by Van Dyck. Below the portrait is the Earl's admiral's baton. The painting is flanked by four Canalettos: two London scenes on the theme of the rebuilding of Westminster Bridge, one of Syon House painted in 1749 and one of Windsor Castle from Percy Lodge, the country seat of the Seventh Duke of Somerset.

## UPPER GUARD CHAMBER

The Upper Guard Chamber was one of the last works to be undertaken in the 19th-century restoration. The Italian architects introduced a style for this vestibule which harmonised with the rest of the interiors.

Giovanni Montiroli designed the marble mosaic floor in the Venetian style and it was laid in the summer of 1864 by the Roman craftsman Luigi Malfatti. The marble balustrade and candelabra flanking the staircase were made in Roman workshops and Giuseppe Nucci, the chief figurative sculptor, carved the figures of Britannia and Justice which stand in alcoves in the east wall.

The ceilings of the Guard Chamber and the staircase are in stucco, the work of William Brien, master plasterer. The arches and groins of the staircase, the panel mouldings and the pier arches dividing the chamber from the staircase carry foliate designs which continue into the mouldings of the Guard Chamber ceiling. The Percy coat of arms decorates the central octagonal coffer.

Opposite hang paintings of the Sixth Duke and Duchess of Somerset by Sir Godfrey Kneller. Below is a pair of landscapes by Orizonte, favourite pictures of the First Duke which had hung at Stanwick Park, his Yorkshire home. Philip de Laszlo's portrait of Helen, Eighth Duchess of Northumberland, was painted in 1916.

Paintings from the Camuccini Collection, purchased by the Fourth Duke in 1854, include Claude's *Sunset*, Lorenzo Lotto's *Infancy Crowning Death*, and Domenico Feti's *Blind Leading the Blind*. Furniture includes two pairs of mid–18th century pier tables and armchairs by the master carver and cabinet maker John Linnell.

LEFT:
PALMA VECCHIO'S
*LADY WITH A LUTE*
HANGS ON THE WEST WALL
OF THE ANTE-LIBRARY

DETAIL FROM PALMA VECCHIO'S
*LADY WITH A LUTE*

# The
# ANTE-LIBRARY

*The Ante-Library is the first room which shows off the craftsmanship of the Alnwick school of carving. Ornamentation carved in pine and gilded was fixed by pins, screws and brackets to the coffered ceiling. The dado is inlaid with sycamore. Four views of Rome by Italian artists, intended to draw attention to the importance of that city to the castle's decorative scheme, were commissioned for this room but they were never hung here.*

Instead, paintings of the Venetian school were hung. *The Lady with a Lute* by Palma Vecchio, the *Triple Portrait* attributed to Titian and the *Artist and his Pupils* by Bernardino Licinio were purchased by the Fourth Duke from the Manfrini Gallery, Venice.

The fresco of *The Visitation* by Sebastiano del Piombo, described by Giorgio Vasari, was purchased by the Duke from the collector Rev. W. Davenport-Bromley in 1853. Titian's *Bishop and his Secretary* was part of the Tenth Earl's collection of Old Masters, which came to him from the collection of the Duke of Buckingham, favourite of Charles I. Of the two which hang alongside it, one, *Ecce Homo*, is by Titian, and the other is attributed to that artist.

Originally the Ante-Library was hung in green Milanese silk.

THE VISITATION
PART OF A FRESCO BY
SEBASTIANO DEL PIOMBO

ECCE HOMO
BY TITIAN

THE BISHOP OF ARMAGNAC
AND HIS SECRETARY
GUILLAUME PHILANDRIER
BY TITIAN

# The
# LIBRARY

*The Library room occupies the principal floor of Salvin's Prudhoe Tower. The bookshelves, in light oak inlaid with sycamore, were installed by George Smith and the coffered ceiling (like all others throughout the state rooms) by the local cabinet maker Thomas Robertson. Giovanni Montiroli designed three trophies with art, music and science as their subjects. The fourth is dedicated to archaeology and the navy, the two main interests of the Fourth Duke.*

Marble busts of Francis Bacon, William Shakespeare and Isaac Newton decorate the three fireplaces.

John Martin, librarian of the Inner Temple, was employed by the Duke to build up his library collection. Extensive purchases at the dispersal sales of collectors and scholars of repute expanded an already distinguished collection. The Ninth Earl (b.1564 d.1632) had assembled one of the finest personal Renaissance libraries in England to help fellow scholars and as a solace during his many years of confinement in the Tower of London. His son Algenon (b.1602 d.1668), who was educated at the Tower, inherited his passion for books. The First Duchess's maternal ancestors, particularly her 'blue stocking' mother Frances Thynne (d.1754) brought numerous choice items to the collection.

GIOVANNI MONTIROLI'S
PEN AND WASH STUDIES FOR
THE LIBRARY CEILING'S TROPHIES

As a patron of the lifeboat movement, the Fourth Duke saw fit to equip his library as a coastal weather station complete with barometer and weather gauges. Daily weather records were maintained and the information passed to national weather records.

Oak library furniture was made by Thomas Robertson.

IN THE BACKGROUND IS THE BUST OF SIR ISAAC NEWTON
BY GIOVANNI STRAZZA c. 1860

WILLIAM SHAKESPEARE
BY FRANCESCO FABI-ALTINI
c. 1860

CARY'S TERRESTRIAL
LIBRARY GLOBE, DATED 1816

The two paintings in the library recess are Sisto Badalocchio's *Erminia and the Shepherds* and *Bacchus and Ariadne* attributed to Nicolas Poussin. In the original scheme of decoration, marble reliefs by McDonald of the Fourth Duke and Duchess decorated the tops of the recess bookshelves. The chandelier, supplied by William Collins in 1822, originally hung in the Great Dining Room of Northumberland House.

GILTWOOD ARMCHAIR, PART OF A LARGE SET SUPPLIED BY MOREL AND HUGHES FOR NORTHUMBERLAND HOUSE IN 1823

PORTRAITS BY SIR PETER LELY OF JOSCELINE PERCY, ELEVENTH EARL OF NORTHUMBERLAND (b.1644 d.1670), AND HIS WIFE LADY ELIZABETH WRIOTHESLEY (d.1690)

Original hangings of Milanese silk, ordered from the silkweaver Ambrosio Osnago in 1864, remain on the walls of the Saloon and Drawing Room. The two pairs of Boulle cabinets were made in Paris for the Saloon under commission from John Webb in 1854. The pair of premier and contre-partie Boulle tables either side of the fireplace date from the early 19th century. Paintings in the Saloon include portraits of the Eleventh Earl and his wife, Elizabeth Wriothesley, by Peter Lely and their daughter Elizabeth, the Percy heiress by Henri Gascars. Portraits of the Tenth Earl and Queen Henrietta Maria are by Van Dyck. Also on the fireplace wall hang two paintings by William Dobson (b.1610 d.1646), recognised as the most important English painter before Hogarth. At each end of the room hang a pair of Canalettos: two Venetian scenes and views of Alnwick Castle and Northumberland House. Other paintings were part of the Camuccini collection.

PORTRAIT OF THE ARTIST WITH NICHOLAS LANIER AND SIR
CHARLES COTTERELL BY WILLIAM DOBSON, c. 1642

*The*
# DRAWING ROOM

*This is the most sumptuous room in the Italian style and the one which fully demonstrates the skills of the decorative designer Giovanni Montiroli in successfully creating a symmetrical design for such an awkwardly-shaped ceiling.*

Alessandro Mantovani painted the frieze of the Drawing Room (and that of the Saloon) in oil on canvas. The frieze was mounted on frames so as to fit the shape of the room. Mantovani spent July and August 1856 at Alnwick supervising this work and working on the background colours of the ceiling. The frieze bears the design of putti, medallions and classical heads in the style used by Guilio Romano for the 16th-century decoration of the Castello di Angelo, Rome, which was an inspiration for the Italian architects in their designs for Alnwick. Carving a pair of lime-wood window shutters occupied one whole year of a craftsman's work-time. Montiroli designed the frames for the overmantel mirrors in the Drawing Room and Saloon which were carved by the Alnwick school.

TWO DETAILS OF THE MARQUETRY
TABLE *c.* 1865 DEPICTING
THE FIVE SENSES

The pair of *pietra-dura* cabinets bear the cypher of Louis XIV and were made at the French king's Gobelins factory for his palace at Versailles in 1683. They are the work of the Florentine craftsman Domenico Cucci. They were purchased by the Third Duke in 1822 from Robert Fogg, a London dealer who supplied furniture to George IV.

The ebonised cabinet was made by Morel and Hughes in 1823 for this same Duke and was designed to house the collection of ivories bought by the First Duchess on her travels abroad in the 1760s and 1770s. The set of Louis XIV-style furniture with tapered cylindrical legs (*c.* 1775-1780) is similar to others designed by Robert Adam.

TWO OF THE IVORY CARVINGS,
BOUGHT BY THE FIRST DUCHESS
ON HER CONTINENTAL TRAVELS

Paintings of the Camuccini collection include Andrea del Sarto's *Portrait of a Young Man*, Guido Reni's *The Crucifixion* and Sisto Badalocchio's *Tancred and Clorinda* and *Rinaldo and Armida*. The distinctive picture frames of the Alnwick school of carving surround the Sisto Badalocchios. There is also J.M.W. Turner's *View of the Temple of Jupiter Panhellenios*, 1816 acquired by the Fourth Duke, a friend of C.R. Cockerell, the architect, who had excavated the temple site in 1811 and advised the Duke on Alnwick's restoration. On the wall opposite hangs Keirincx's *Orpheus and the Thracian Women* (right), which the First Duchess records in her journal (*c.* 1770) as being purchased by her in the Low Countries for £12.1s.6d!

# The
# DINING ROOM

*The Great Hall* had been at the centre of castle life in medieval times. Rearrangements of rooms in the 18th century did not lessen its importance. It had daily use by the family when resident: the alcove was used for breakfasting. It was here also that the First Duke and Duchess entertained local gentry and worthies on their open days. On such occasions the Duchess had her piper play to the guests from beneath the dining room windows in the inner bailey.

Mantovani's scheme for a painted frieze for this room was not accepted so its decoration fell to the school of carving whose panels of garlanded heraldic motifs and intervening stylised cornucopias of fruits created the school's masterpiece. The ceiling, carved in Brunswick pine, left ungilded, is decorated with the heraldry of Percy. It replaced an 18th century heraldic ceiling in plaster.

The room was lit by two candelabra wound down through trap doors in the ceiling, either side of the central coffer, to hang above the dining table. The great fireplace, exhibited in Italy by Taccalozzi before it was sent to Alnwick, takes up the heraldic theme in its frieze celebrating the Fourth Duke and his Duchess in the badges of Percy and Grosvenor.

AN ARMORIAL DESIGN BY MONTIROLI FOR THE CEILING

TUREEN FROM MEISSEN
DINNER SERVICE *c.* 1745
AND PLATE FROM LATER
MEISSEN DINNER SERVICE
ILLUSTRATED WITH
AESOP'S FABLES, *c.* 1780

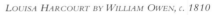

CORNER SECTION OF CARVED FRIEZE

LOUISA HARCOURT BY WILLIAM OWEN, *c.* 1810

The buffets and side tables were made locally in the
workshops of the cabinet maker Thomas Robertson.
The seat furniture includes a set of dining chairs and a set of
side chairs with two armchairs which in the 18th century
had been at the First Duke's family seat of Stanwick Hall.
The table silver includes the plateau made by Edward
Thomason in 1818 to a design by the Third Duchess and
the silver-gilt candelabra and cups form part of the service
created by the London silversmiths, Rundell, Bridge and
Rundell 1822-1830.

Over the fireplace hang portraits of the First Duke and
Duchess in a frame by the Alnwick school. On the
southern wall hangs the portrait of the Fourth Duke in
admiral's uniform by Sir Francis Grant. To the right, above
the door, hangs the portrait of Louisa Harcourt by William
Owen. Louisa romantically and clandestinely married the
young Lord Lovaine in 1801. She died in 1848 but he lived
on to succeed his cousin to the ducal title in 1865 at
the age of 87. This duke's portrait by Gustav
Pope hangs on the north wall.
From this marriage alliance the
present Percy line descends.

DETAIL OF A HAND-PAINTED PLATTER FROM
THE GREAT MEISSEN DINNER SERVICE,
DEPICTING A RHINOCEROS

# The
# BREAKFAST ROOM

*This room was untouched by the mid-19th century restoration but by the 1890s the late Gothic hammer roof was falling to pieces. Eustace Balfour, the architect, restored the room in Queen Anne style for the Sixth Duke. The flat stucco ceiling is decorated with the heraldic design of the crescent and the fetterlock. The wall covering is heavily embossed paper which imitates leather. The fireplace surround is of fossilised marble; within it is an ancient armorial grate.*

The collector's cabinet formerly belonged to the naturalist and ornithologist Prideaux Selby, famous for his illustrated books on native birds, who lived at Twizell House north of Alnwick and whose elder brother was the duke's commissioner at the end of the 18th century. The 18th century painted canvas is part of a set by the French artist Clermont once used to decorate the marquees at Syon House when the First Duchess held her fêtes.

The pair of paintings either side of the fireplace are attributed to Peter Hartover who worked in the years 1674–1690. They depict the castles of Alnwick (pictured below) and Warkworth. The Alnwick painting provides the most detailed illustration of the castle before its 18th century restoration; it also provides a south view of the town showing such landmarks as Bondgate Tower, the Tollbooth and Alnwick Abbey outside the town. This room is now used for temporary exhibitions.

Alnwick Castle

*The*

# PICTURE GALLERY

*This gallery constructed by Salvin contains family portraits, including Lord Algernon Percy, younger son of the First Duke, by Batoni, and the Fourth Duke when a midshipman by Phillips. The Fourth Duke who served on various stations in the Napoleonic Wars commissioned the historical painting of a naval action against the French by the artist Luny.*

HMS CALEDONIAN AND HMS BOYNE CHASING
THE FRENCH FLEET IN BOULOGNE, BY THOMAS LUNY, 1830

At the time of the Peace of Amiens (1802) the Second Duke sent his favourite artist Thomas Phillips to Paris to paint Napoleon; the unfinished portrait of Wellington by George Dawe is its pendant. The northern marine artist Carmichael was patronized by the Fourth Duke who was Treasurer of the Royal Lifeboat Institute and awarded a prize for the invention of the first self-righting lifeboat.

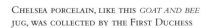

CHELSEA PORCELAIN, LIKE THIS *GOAT AND BEE*
JUG, WAS COLLECTED BY THE FIRST DUCHESS

A number of portraits are of members of the Drummond family. They set up a prosperous banking business in London in the early 18th century. In May 1845 Algernon George Percy, later Sixth Duke of Northumberland, married Louisa Drummond who became sole heiress of her father's estate which included Albury, Surrey. This remains in the possession of the Percys.

*ELIZABETH DRUMMOND* (b.1734 d.1819), ANCESTOR
OF THE SIXTH DUCHESS OF NORTHUMBERLAND
BY THOMAS GAINSBOROUGH

# *The*
# CHAPEL

*This room is a mid-19th century addition* to the keep by the architect
*Anthony Salvin and combines English Victorian gothic with Italian art in its internal decoration.
In the Middle Ages the Percy household was a bustle with the activities of priests and clerics;
taking divine service, praying for the souls of past Percy lords, taking care of the muniments and
libraries and keeping the household accounts. The household could not have functioned without its
men of the cloth. Throughout the many Percy baronies, patronage and material support
were offered to monastries, secular clergy, hermits, chantry priests, scholars and teachers.*

Here at Alnwick canons and friars of two religious houses
within the parklands received Percy support, so did a
considerable chantry established in what is now the parish
church. In addition, a chantry served by three priests was
established at the castle in the middle of the 14th century to
pray for Percy souls and to run a school. Its chapel was built
in the inner bailey close to the Constable's Tower. The
ruined and stripped gable ends of this chapel survived into
the 18th century and are shown in Canaletto's painting of
the castle.

The remains of this medieval chapel were swept away in the
restoration work of the First Duke and Duchess. Robert
Adam completed the restoration of the castle in the early
1780s with the building of a library room and chapel on the
principal level of the new castle wing which stretched from
the keep to the Middle Gateway. The chapel occupied
the eastern part of this building, above the gateway
itself. Adam decorated the walls of the chapel with the
Percy family tree and placed within it a sarcophagus
as a memorial to the First Duchess. He also designed
a lectern and priest's chair, now on display here,
recognised as among his finest furniture in the
late *gothick* style.

This furniture is all that remains of Adam's chapel
which disappeared in the restoration of the
mid-19th century. While the old library and chapel

were transformed into a principal suite of rooms for the Fourth Duke and Duchess, the architect Anthony Salvin was left in something of a quandary concerning the siting of a new chapel. He produced one design of a freestanding chapel close to the Middle Gateway in the inner bailey; and another of a freestanding chapel sited in the outer bailey. In the end, economy and convenience won the day, and the chapel was incorporated in the fabric of the restored keep on its south side.

The chapel's gothic ceiling and lancet windows are in keeping with Salvin's design for the ground floor of the castle; its mosaic marble walls are of Italian design and manufacture and complement the Italian style so pronounced in the castle's principal rooms. It is only here in the chapel that both styles are brought together. The decoration of the stone bosses of the roof groins are the work of the eminent sculptor James Forsyth of London.

Salvin's chapel offered a daily opportunity for family members and household staff, to come together for a common act of worship. The ducal party entered the gallery of the chapel on the principal level directly from the state rooms. Below the gallery, at ground level, the servants assembled in their pews from the different servants' halls. Household rules obliged all servants whose duties allowed to attend prayers at 8am.

*358*

Mr DUTENS TUTOR TO LORD ALGERNON PERCY

In the Sixth Duke's time (1867-1899) the form of the service was set out in a published book of family prayers.

It was the duty of the duke's chaplain to lead family prayers. The chaplain usually had other responsibilities, such as ministry of the local church or the duties of duke's secretary or tutor to his children. Services regularly took place in the chapel until the 1970s including family marriage and baptism.

LOUIS DUTENS (*b.* 1730 *d.* 1812), RECTOR OF ELSDON, NORTHUMBERLAND; TUTOR TO ALGERNON, YOUNGER SON OF THE FIRST DUKE AND DUCHESS, DURING HIS GRAND TOUR 1768-1771

Part of the Fourth Duke's haul of treasures from his travels in Italy and on the Continent in the 1860s included the French tapestries which now cover the Chapel walls. He placed them in the suite of rooms which Salvin restored for him at Warkworth Castle. It was not until the 1960s that they were hung in the chapel at Alnwick Castle. Two of the tapestries, made in Paris *circa* 1625, show scenes from the life of Constantine the Great, the first Christian emperor: one his baptism, the other his vision. The five mid-18th century Aubusson tapestries tell the biblical story of the blind Tobit and his dutiful son Tobias who finds the cure for his father's blindness.

THOMAS PERCY (*b.* 1729 *d.* 1811), ANTIQUARIAN, POET, SCHOLAR; CHAPLAIN TO THE FIRST DUKE AND DUCHESS OF NORTHUMBERLAND, LATER BISHOP OF DROMORE

LEFT: THE WALLS OF THE CHAPEL ARE COVERED WITH THE FOURTH DUKE'S FRENCH TAPESTRIES, BROUGHT BACK FROM HIS TRAVELS AROUND THE CONTINENT IN THE 1860'S

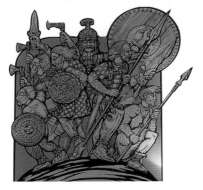

*'Forging Power'*

# The Dukes and their
# MUSEUM

*'Recording of*
*Egyptian*
*inscriptions'*

*The Castle Museum, opened to the public in 1826, played a full part in the Fourth Duke's scheme of restoration. It was his intention to promote the serious study of the archaeology of the North and he surrounded himself with the keenest and best informed minds for that purpose. Under his patronage important investigations and digs were undertaken; the number of artefacts increased through his own enthusiastic collecting and purchasing; and the process of cataloguing the collection was begun. Archaeological digs continue to take place on estate lands today, adding new finds to the collection.*

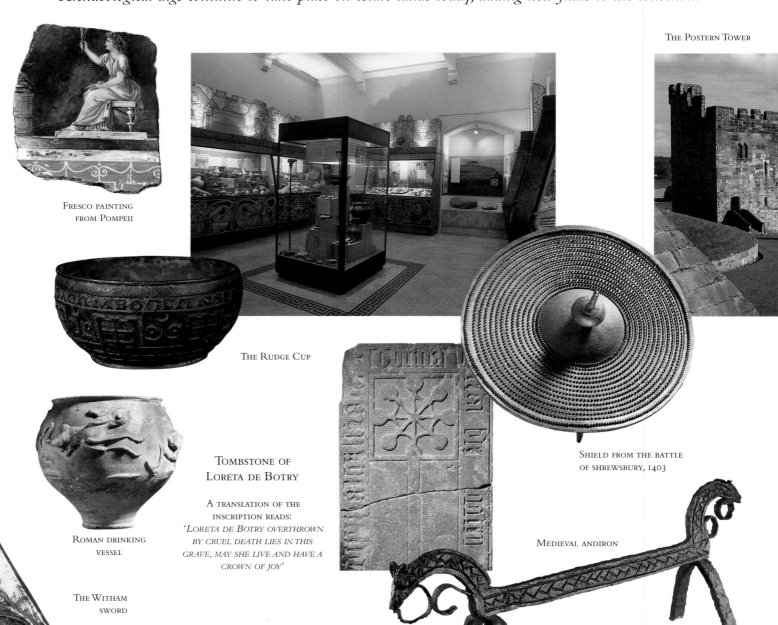

THE POSTERN TOWER

Fresco painting
from Pompeii

The Rudge Cup

Shield from the battle
of shrewsbury, 1403

Tombstone of
Loreta de Botry

A translation of the
inscription reads:
'Loreta de Botry overthrown
by cruel death lies in this
grave, may she live and have a
crown of joy'

Roman drinking
vessel

The Witham
sword

Medieval andiron

## Constable's Tower
# *Percy Tenantry Volunteers*
# EXHIBITION

*No single act in Percy history* demonstrates better the workings of a great landed estate, *the interplay of characters and events and the fusing of national and local concerns, than the raising of these military volunteers at the time of danger of Napoleonic invasion. Models of members of the force shown here are based on real-life persons whose records survive among the papers of the Percy Tenantry Volunteers (1798-1814).*

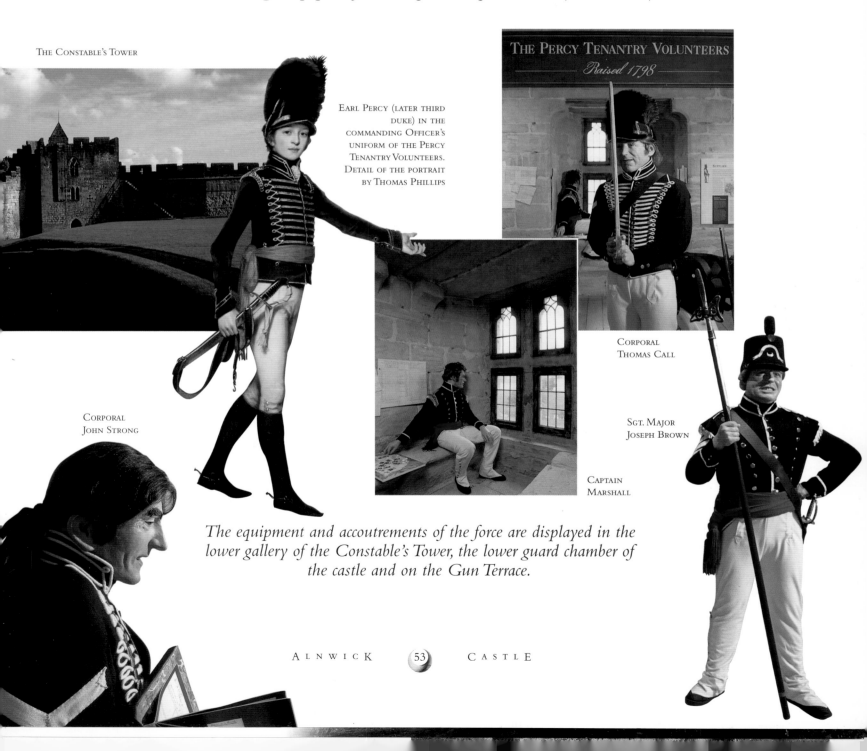

THE CONSTABLE'S TOWER

EARL PERCY (LATER THIRD DUKE) IN THE COMMANDING OFFICER'S UNIFORM OF THE PERCY TENANTRY VOLUNTEERS. DETAIL OF THE PORTRAIT BY THOMAS PHILLIPS

CORPORAL THOMAS CALL

CORPORAL JOHN STRONG

SGT. MAJOR JOSEPH BROWN

CAPTAIN MARSHALL

*The equipment and accoutrements of the force are displayed in the lower gallery of the Constable's Tower, the lower guard chamber of the castle and on the Gun Terrace.*

*Alnwick Castle and Hulne Park* are amongst the most filmed locations in the north and have played host to many film and television productions over the years. These include **Becket** with Peter O'Toole and Richard Burton; **Mary Queen of Scots** with Vanessa Redgrave; **Ivanhoe** with Anthony Andrews and Sam Neil; **Robin Hood – Prince of Thieves** with Kevin Costner; the award-winning production of **Elizabeth** with Cate Blanchett and Joseph Fiennes; and most recently **Harry Potter and the Philosopher's Stone** and **Harry Potter and The Chamber of Secrets.**

A SCENE FROM THE FAMOUS *HARRY POTTER AND THE PHILOSOPHER'S STONE*

Television has used the facilities for a diverse range of productions, such as *The Antiques Roadshow, Treasure Hunt, The Clothes Show* and *Highway* as well as *Robin of Sherwood, Blackadder, The Fast Show* and several episodes of popular *Catherine Cookson* series.

SCENES IN *ELIZABETH*: OF CARNAGE ON THE
BANKS OF THE RIVER ALN (ABOVE);
AND THE TRANSFORMED
INNER BAILEY (RIGHT)

THE INNER
COURTYARD
PLAYS HOST TO
YOUNG ARTHUR
WITHDRAWING
EXCALIBUR
FROM THE
STONE;
A SCENE FROM
*THE DARK
KNIGHT*

HULNE ABBEY DRESSED AS
MAID MARION'S HOUSE
FOR THE HOLLYWOOD FEATURE
*ROBIN HOOD -
PRINCE OF THIEVES,*
STARRING KEVIN COSTNER

*Alnwick Castle and Hulne Park provide an enormous
variety of educational resources*
including art, archaeology, architecture, farming, forestry, environmental
conservation, tourism, military and social history.
*An education programme is run by the estate
using these resources.*